Psalm 23

DEVOTIONAL AND STUDY GUIDE FOR INDIVIDUALS AND GROUPS

by ROXANNE DRURY

For my Lord and Savior,

Jesus of Nazareth.

Lectio Divina

Lectio Divina[1] is a method of studying Scripture that dates back to the 3rd century. It has monastic roots as a practice of reading, meditating, and praying through Scripture with the "intention of communion with God." The goal of using this method of Bible study is to increase the reader's knowledge and understanding of God's Word. Lectio Divina in Latin literally means "divine reading" or "spiritual reading."

The four steps of Lectio Divina are: Read, Meditate, Pray, and Contemplate. In this study the steps have been adapted to 5-R's: Read, Reflect, Respond, Rest, and Remember. Each step is intended to guide a separate part of a person's being.

READ ~ HEART   REFLECT ~ MIND   RESPOND ~ SPIRIT

REST ~ BODY   REMEMBER ~ SOUL

The 5-R's method of Bible Study is a slow and steady study of the Word. Take your time walking on your journey through Psalm 23.

Guided by the Holy Spirit we'll engage in the full measure of scripture as we pray **"Show me your ways, O Lord, teach me your paths; guide me in your truth and teach me, for you are God my Savior, and my hope is in you all day long."**

Psalm 25:4-5

---

1 Lectio Divina. (2022, November 16). In Wikipedia. Https://En.wikipedia.org/Wiki/Lectio_divina

How we will study

LECTIO DIVINA: The spiritual practice of divine reading.

Read (Heart)	Read the passage to yourself twice. **What does the passage say that I should understand?**
Reflect (Mind)	Reflect on the word. **Think about the words and pinpoint a word or phrase that speaks to you.**
Respond (Spirit)	Personal prayer time. **What can I say to the Lord in response?**
Rest (Body)	Rest in the Word and perhaps write the Scripture in your journal as well as your thoughts feelings and prayers. **Rest in the presence of the Lord.**
Remember (Soul)	Memorization. **The goal will be to memorize Psalm 23.**

HOW TO MAKE THE MOST OF THE PSALM 23 DEVOTIONAL AND STUDY GUIDE AS AN INDIVIDUAL STUDY:

+ Have ready your Bible, a pen, and a journal to record your thoughts and what is in your heart.
+ Read the verse twice, read the Devotional and then follow the instructions given.
+ You can work through each verse over a week's time for a six week study or you can work through the study over six days or however long you desire.

HOW TO MAKE THE MOST OF THE PSALM 23 DEVOTIONAL AND STUDY GUIDE AS A GROUP STUDY:

- The 6-week format lends itself best to a group study.
- Group studies will take approximately half an hour once a week.
- Each person has ready a Bible, pen and a journal.
- The leader will explain Lectio Divina and how this study will work at the first Group Time.
- The leader will read the Introduction to the Group followed by the Prayer and a Group Reading of Psalm 23.
- Each week, The Group reads the Verse twice together and the leader reads the Devotional.
- The balance of the work is done at home through the week by the participants. Participants can be encouraged to reread the verse and devotional.
- The next week the leader facilitates the Group Discussion questions and anyone from the group may share what they learned over the week.
- And then the group repeats the steps of reading the next verse twice and the leader reading the Devotional. And so on for the 6 weeks.

Introduction

Psalm 23 is a beloved portion of scripture for people of all ages. Psalm 23 was written by David as an expression of his complete trust in God and His loving care. Some theologians say David may have composed the Psalm while he was still a shepherd boy watching his father's flocks. It is also suggested he may have been on the same Shepherd Field where, 1,000 years later, the angel choir announced the birth of Jesus.[1] Still other scholars believe because of the calm nature and maturity exhibited in the words of Psalm 23 that it was written while David was king. He may have been reminiscing about his boyhood as a shepherd. As a shepherd, David was well aware of what shepherding involved. A shepherd feeds and leads his sheep. A shepherd makes sure his sheep have all the essentials needed to live—like grass and water. If a sheep wanders, the shepherd tracks him down and brings him back to the fold. A shepherd keeps his flock safe from harm. Psalm 23 speaks directly to us with a message of comfort and reassurance that:

- ◆ God loves you
- ◆ God will care for you
- ◆ God can be trusted
- ◆ God wants you to be with Him forever one day

In Psalm 23, we can identify God as our shepherd, the be-all and end-all in meeting every need. God knows you by name and He knows all you are going through or ever will go through. He will be right there with you through it all, just as He was with David.

My prayer is that you will get much out of this study. So, open your heart and mind and have fun following the Lord your shepherd!

1 Reference: Haley's Bible Handbook, Zondervan Publishing House, 1965, pg 255

Prayer

"Show me your ways, O Lord, teach me your paths;
Guide me in your truth and teach me, for you are God my Savior,
and my hope is in you all day long."
Psalm 25: 4 & 5, Amen.

Psalm 23: A Psalm of David

1 The LORD is my shepherd;
I shall not want.
2 He makes me lie down in green pastures,
He leads me beside still waters.
3 He restores my soul.
He guides me in paths of righteousness
For His name's sake.
4 Even though I walk through the valley
of the shadow of death,
I will fear no evil,
for You are with me;
Your rod and Your staff,
they comfort me.
5 You prepare a table before me
in the presence of my enemies;
You anoint my head with oil;
my cup overflows.
6 Surely goodness and love will follow me
all the days of my life,
and I will dwell in the
House of the LORD forever."

Verse 1

1 *The Lord is my shepherd; I shall not want.*

DEVOTIONAL:

A Psalm is a sacred song or poem used in worship according to the Merriam-Webster dictionary. David wrote this Psalm when he was a man but he was a shepherd as a child. Undoubtedly these words held much meaning for him. Being a shepherd was an important but lowly job. Interesting that David was chosen to be the king. The 23rd Psalm is probably one of the most well-known of all the Psalms in the Bible. Most people believe Psalm 23 was written when David was king. It is as relevant for us today as it was for David. God knows all the things you face in your life and He is right there with you. I believe David wrote this Psalm not only for himself as an act of worship, but for all believers to know that God is with us always—taking care of us as a shepherd would take care of his sheep. We will come to understand how He responds to our needs as we walk through each verse during this study.

DO: Go ahead and circle the words "is" and "my" in the verse above.
   "Is" and "my" make this sentence a statement, not a question.

The Lord IS David's shepherd. That implies that David has a relationship with the Lord.

DO: Re-read verse 1 with emphasis on IS and then read it again
   with emphasis on MY.

Claiming God as his own makes David confident that he has all he needs according to God's will for him. It is very personal and shows a high level of trust in God.

REFLECT:

- Read verse 1 quietly to yourself twice.
- Write down the word or phrase that spoke to you from this verse.

_____

_____

_____

- Why did it have meaning for you?

_____

_____

_____

_____

_____

_____

_____

RESPOND:

Re-read verse 1 and replace your name for each of the personal pronouns.

REST:

Resting in God's Word is a valuable tool in helping to understand its meaning and how it applies to your life in whatever season you are in right now.

DO THIS:

1. Pray quietly and ask God to reveal Himself to you in the words we are studying.
2. Date the top of a fresh journal page.
3. Write the scripture verse in your journal.
4. Write down anything that comes to mind as a prayer of thanks or praise.

SUGGESTED ADDITIONAL STEPS TO TAKE IN YOUR JOURNALING TIME:

1. Remembering that you are created in the image of a very creative God, take time to draw or write what the verse brings to mind. Use your imagination.

2. Write down your thoughts from when you were drawing or reading the scripture or refer to notes you wrote. What were you thinking about God? What do you want to say to Him? Did He speak to you?

3. **Other things to consider:**
    *   Do you think of Him as your shepherd?
    *   How is your relationship with Him?
    *   Do you recognize that He supplies all of your needs? How should you respond to that?

REMEMBER:

Take time this week to repeat verse 1 to yourself or out loud several times to commit it to memory.

GROUP DISCUSSION:

*   How did reading/saying your own name in this verse make it different from when you first read it?
*   What comes to mind when you think of the term "shepherd"?
*   Share insights and thoughts.

Notes:

Verse 2

2 *He makes me lie down in green pastures,*
He leads me beside still waters.

DEVOTIONAL:

Rest is good! A green pasture sounds very gentle and like a place of peace. Peace is good! Close your eyes and imagine yourself in the middle of a beautiful green pasture. How do you feel? The phrase "He leads me beside still waters" has a very specific meaning for sheep and a shepherd. The shepherd is responsible for the care of the flock. Rest, food, and water are their primary needs. Some waters are slow-moving and some are fast-moving. If a shepherd takes his sheep to fast-moving water, they won't drink. They are afraid of the motion and the sound. The shepherd must find a slow-moving stream for his sheep to be refreshed.

This is what God does for you. He takes action to give you what you need. He takes action to care for you. Why? Because He loves you. He wants to care for you as a shepherd does his sheep. When you go to Him, He gives you rest and refreshment in a peaceful pasture. So, climb into His loving arms and rest. Be at peace on the lap of the God who is your good shepherd.

REFLECT:

♦ Read verse 2 quietly to yourself twice.

♦ Write down the word or phrase that spoke to you from this verse.

_____

_____

_____

♦ Why did it have meaning for you?

_____

_____

_____

_____

_____

_____

_____

RESPOND:

Reread verse 2 and replace the word "me" with your name.

REST:

Resting in God's Word is a valuable tool in helping to understand its meaning and how it applies to your life in whatever season you are in right now.

DO THIS:

1. Pray quietly and ask God to reveal Himself to you in the words we are studying.
2. Date the top of a fresh journal page.
3. Write the scripture verse in your journal.
4. Write down anything that comes to mind as a prayer of thanks or praise.

SUGGESTED ADDITIONAL STEPS TO TAKE IN YOUR JOURNALING TIME:

1. Remembering that you are created in the image of a very creative God, take time to draw or write what the verse brings to mind. Use your imagination.

2. Write down your thoughts from when you were drawing or reading the scripture or refer to notes you wrote. What were you thinking about God? What do you want to say to Him? Did He speak to you? What did He reveal?

3. **Other things to consider:**
   - How is your relationship with Him?
   - When was the last time you rested in the presence of God? Did you hear His voice?

REMEMBER:

Take time this week to repeat verse 2 to yourself or out loud several times to commit it to memory.

GROUP DISCUSSION:

- Have you seen times of rest that God has provided or forced on you where you were refreshed? Acknowledge His provision by sharing with the group?
- Do you need rest and refreshment from God right now?
- Share insights and thoughts.

Notes:

Verse 3

3 He restores my soul. He guides me in paths of righteousness for His name's sake.

DEVOTIONAL:

The word restore means to make right again or put back the way it should be. In this passage we find healing. The Shepherd, the Lord, heals your soul—the very essence of who you are. If you are hurt or sad, confused or lonely, overwhelmed or depressed, anxious, worried or troubled, God restores your soul to the way it should be. Just ask! This is just one more way He cares for you as a shepherd would care for his sheep. If you stray from God, He will look for you. He loves you that much!

He is your guide back to full health—physical, mental, and spiritual. He shows you the path and prepares the way by giving you all you need to bring Him glory in your healing. He will never lead you where He cannot care for you. He calls you to just follow. He is waiting to restore you and guide you. Praise His name.

REFLECT:
- Read verse 3 quietly to yourself twice.
- Write down the word or phrase that spoke to you from this verse.

_____

_____

_____

- Why did it have meaning for you?

_____

_____

_____

_____

_____

_____

_____

RESPOND:
Re-read verse 3 and put yourself in this verse. Make it personal.

REST:
Resting in God's Word is a valuable tool in helping to understand its meaning and how it applies to your life in whatever season you are in right now.

DO THIS:
1. Pray quietly and ask God to reveal Himself to you in the words we are studying.
2. Date the top of a fresh journal page.
3. Write the scripture verse in your journal.
4. Write down anything that comes to mind as a prayer of thanks or praise.

SUGGESTED ADDITIONAL STEPS TO TAKE IN YOUR JOURNALING TIME:

1. Write a specific prayer asking for God to guide you in a specific way.
2. **Other things to consider:**
    *   Are you seeing God provide for you?
    *   Are you relying on God as a sheep relies on the shepherd?
    *   Is your heart heavy or hurting? Do you need to ask for healing?

REMEMBER:

Take time this week to repeat verse 3 to yourself or out loud several times to commit it to memory.

GROUP DISCUSSION:

*   Have you ever experienced God's healing or restoration?
*   Have you ever experienced God's leading? Did you follow? If not, why? How did God equip you?
*   How can you make a life-change based on the verses we have studied thus far? What has spoken to you personally.

Notes:

Verse 4

4 Even though I walk through the valley of the shadow of death, I will fear no evil, for you are with me; Your rod and Your staff, they comfort me.

DEVOTIONAL:

Beginning with this verse, David changes the pronoun from 'He' to 'You'. Instead of talking ABOUT God, David is talking TO God, his shepherd. This changes our perspective and shows the intimacy that David has with God. He now speaks directly to Him. God wants that intimacy with you. He made you for a relationship with Him. He says in His word, "Come to me, all you who labor and are heavy laden and I will give you rest." Matthew 11:28 "I will fear no evil for YOU are with me." David faced a giant without fear. He killed a lion without fear. The same God that was with David is with you. The same God that protected David is protecting you. The same God that gave David rest and peace is with you. Take in these words, **He is with you!**

A shepherd carried a few tools with him as he watched over the sheep. A rod and a staff. The rod was used to protect his sheep from predators. It was a weapon. The staff was used to guide, correct, and perhaps discipline a wayward or ornery sheep. When someone cares about you as the shepherd does his sheep, they protect, they guide, they correct, and even discipline. David was comforted by God's protection, guidance, correction, and discipline. How often do you get bent out of shape at correction or discipline? No, it is comforting to know someone, God, anyone, cares and loves you enough to protect, guide, correct, and discipline. He walks with you through every storm, He will not let you do it alone and if correction and guidance are needed to get you through that storm, trust Him enough to accept that. Will you?

REFLECT:

- Read verse 4 quietly to yourself twice.
- Write down the word or phrase that spoke to you from this verse.

_____

_____

_____

- Why did it have meaning for you?

_____

_____

_____

_____

_____

_____

_____

RESPOND:

Re-read verse 4 and and recognize that as you read it you are speaking to the Almighty God, our Heavenly Father who loves you unconditionally. He loves you enough to protect, guide, correct and discipline you.

REST:

Resting in God's Word is a valuable tool in helping to understand its meaning and how it applies to your life in whatever season you are in right now.

DO THIS:

1. Pray quietly and ask God to reveal Himself to you in the words we are studying.
2. Date the top of a fresh journal page.
3. Write the scripture verse in your journal.
4. Write down anything that comes to mind as a prayer of thanks or praise.

SUGGESTED ADDITIONAL STEPS TO TAKE IN YOUR JOURNALING TIME:

1. Read the following verses: Hebrews 4:14-16, 10:23 and 13:5 & 6.

2. Write down your thoughts on God's faithfulness. Find one verse in the Bible that speaks to God's faithfulness. Pray a prayer of adoration to God for His faithfulness?

3. **Other things to consider:**
    ◆   Are you dealing with a valley right now?
    ◆   Have you brought it to God? You can do that right now?
    ◆   Write a prayer of thanksgiving for God's protection, guidance, and even His correction and discipline.

REMEMBER:

Take time this week to repeat verse 4 to yourself or out loud several times to commit it to memory.

GROUP DISCUSSION:

◆   Someone read Hebrews 4:14-16. Discuss. What do these verses mean to you personally?

◆   Look up the word "worry" in the concordance of your Bible. We will each read out a verse we find.

Notes:

Verse 5

5 *You prepare a table before me in the presence of my enemies; You anoint my head with oil; my cup overflows.*

DEVOTIONAL:

God prepares a feast for His faithful children. He provides all good things for you to enjoy so everyone can see the very perfect picture of His love. Know this—He delights in you. I repeat—God delights in YOU!

He chose you—He anoints your head with the oil of His love. The anointing with oil was symbolic. It meant you were chosen, consecrated, and commissioned for a holy task. David in verse 5 was proclaiming that God had called him out for a sacred job—that of King. The Lord calls every believer to a sacred job as well—that of sharing the gospel, that of being light in a dark world, that of bringing glory to God. You are called to a sacred job. You—are—anointed with the oil of His love.

"My cup overflows." Verse 1 of Psalm 23 states that the Lord gives His people what they need. Verse 5 says then He gives more and more and more—an abundance. He has an abundance for you. Whatever that looks like to you. The cool thing is that God's blessing is not limited to material things, it also includes access to the Holy Spirit. Read Luke 11:13. The Holy Spirit is a good gift God has given you. When you have doubts, fears, and worries, remember who you belong to. Remember who your Father is. You are a child of the King.

REFLECT:

- Read verse 5 quietly to yourself twice.
- Write down the word or phrase that spoke to you from this verse.

_____

_____

_____

- Why did it have meaning for you?

_____

_____

_____

_____

_____

_____

_____

RESPOND:

You have been anointed with the oil of God's love. You have been chosen, commissioned, consecrated and called out for a sacred job. In your journal, write about how that makes you feel.

REST:

Resting in God's Word is a valuable tool in helping to understand its meaning and how it applies to your life in whatever season you are in right now.

DO THIS:

1. Pray quietly and ask God to reveal Himself to you in the words we are studying.
2. Date the top of a fresh journal page.
3. Write the scripture verse in your journal.
4. Write down anything that comes to mind as a prayer of thanks or praise.
5. If you are unsure of your call, ask God to reveal it to you.

SUGGESTED ADDITIONAL STEPS TO TAKE IN YOUR JOURNALING TIME:

1. Read Ephesians 3:20.
2. How does this verse coincide with verse 5 of Psalm 23? Write about that.
3. **Other things to consider:**
   - Is the cup in this verse referring to a literal cup or something else? What things in your life are overflowing? In a good way or a bad way?
   - Have you brought it to God? You can do that right now?
   - Write a prayer thanking God for being for you. Thank Him for inviting you into the life He has planned for you.

REMEMBER:

Take time this week to repeat verse 5 to yourself or out loud several times to commit it to memory.

GROUP DISCUSSION:

- Someone read John 10:10. Discuss. What does having life to the full mean for you personally?
- Read Ephesians 3:20. Discuss. What abundance has God given you that surpassed what you could have imagined possible?

Notes:

Verse 6

6 Surely goodness and love will follow me all the days of my life, And I will dwell in the house of the Lord forever.

DEVOTIONAL:

Goodness is a part of who God is. It is part of His nature. Everything God does is loving and good. He chases after you all the days of your life because of His goodness and His love for you. You can say then that your life is filled with God's goodness and love because He cares so very much for you. That is His blessing in your life. Being chosen, consecrated, for His purposes is part of His blessing on your life. This doesn't mean everything in your life will be perfect. It means that God's goodness and love will always be with you. Knowing this, you can lean into it when you need to and He will be there.

Read Romans 8:38 & 39—Contemplate these words for a moment. Soak them in and feel all the feels about the fact that NOTHING—absolutely NOTHING—can separate you from God's love. Always will He love you. Always!

REFLECT:

- Read verse 6 quietly to yourself twice.
- Write down the word or phrase that spoke to you from this verse.

_____

_____

_____

- Why did it have meaning for you?

_____

_____

_____

RESPOND:

- Re-read verse 6 and rest in the verse for a moment.
- Name 2 people you absolutely love.

_____   _____

- Name 2 people that absolutely love you.

_____   _____

- Why do you love them and why do they love you? How do you show love and how do they show love to you? _____

_____

_____

_____

_____

_____

- Identify ways that God shows love to you. _____

_____

_____

_____

_____

_____

REST:

Resting in God's Word is a valuable tool in helping to understand its meaning and how it applies to your life in whatever season you are in right now.

DO THIS:

1. Pray quietly and ask God to reveal Himself to you in the words we are studying.
2. Date the top of a fresh journal page.
3. Write the scripture verse in your journal.
4. Write down anything that comes to mind as a prayer of thanks or praise.

SUGGESTED ADDITIONAL STEPS TO TAKE IN YOUR JOURNALING TIME:

1. Read the following verses: Romans 8:38 & 39, Romans 5:8.
2. Write down your thoughts on God's love for you.
3. **Other things to consider:**
   - How has God gifted you with His goodness and love in your life?
   - If goodness and love have come to you through the people in your life, have you thanked them?
   - Write a prayer thanking and praising God for His goodness and love?

REMEMBER:

Take time this week to repeat verse 6 to yourself or out loud several times to commit it to memory.

GROUP DISCUSSION:

- What are your thoughts on David saying he will dwell in the house of the Lord forever?
- As we conclude our study of Psalm 23, which of the 6 verses had the most impact on you? How and why?

Notes:

Closing Verses

Read the following verses to yourself or aloud as a group. Allow them to wash over you and fill you with the same confidence in God that David had as he wrote Psalm 23. He is the same God today as He was then.

"The faithful love of the Lord never ends!
His mercies never cease.
Great is His faithfulness;
His mercies begin afresh each morning."
Lamentations 3:22-23 NLT

"When I think of all this, I fall to my knees and pray to the Father, the Creator of everything in heaven and on earth. I pray that from His glorious, unlimited resources He will empower you with inner strength through His Spirit. Then Christ will make His home in your hearts as you trust in Him. Your roots will grow down into God's love and keep you strong. And may you have the power to understand, as all God's people should, how wide, how long, how high, and how deep His love is. May you experience the love of Christ, though it is too great to understand fully. Then you will be made complete with all the fullness of life and power that comes from God."
Ephesians 3:14-19 NLT

Do You Know
The Shepherd?

It could be that after going through this study you are unsure if you know, truly know, the Shepherd as David did. David had a personal relationship with the Lord and you can too. God is waiting for you to come to Him. He loves you with a love that is immeasurable and unconditional. Everyone makes wrong choices now and again and God knows that. He made us. Admit to Him your wrong choices and ask His forgiveness. God's Word promises in 1 John 1 :9 "If we confess our sins, He is faithful and just and will forgive us our sins and cleanse us from all unrighteousness." You can believe that He is faithful and just to forgive. Then ask Him to come into your life and be your Lord and Savior. He will. He longs to have a relationship with you because He loves you. He loved you enough to die for you.

YOU CAN PRAY THESE WORDS: God, I have made wrong choices in my life please forgive me and come into my life. I am asking you to be my Lord and Savior and be with me all my days. Thank you for loving me and accepting me just as I am. Amen.

About the Author

Roxanne Drury is a teacher, writer, and bestselling author who loves the Lord, His Word, and His people. Her passion is the discipleship of the young and the old. This combination inspires her to create materials that draw people closer to God and guide them to find a personal application in His Word.

She is a bestselling children's book author, contributing author to Christian Living magazine, and author and facilitator of several Bible studies.

A veteran in the field of Christian education, Roxanne currently writes the Bible teaching curriculum for the ministry to children at her local church. She lives in Meridian, Idaho with her husband, Steve, and their dog Daisy. She has four grown children and six grandchildren.

Jodi McPhee currently lives in the Pacific Northwest. Her background in book publishing led her to become the creative wizard that brings beauty and design to the pages of the books she formats. Many thanks to Jodi for her exquisite interior and cover design of the *Psalm 23 Devotional and Study Guide for Individuals and Groups.*

Acknowledgments:

Many thanks to my support and encouragement network of friends who walked through the Psalm 23 Devotional and Study Guide with me: Andrea, Charla, Katie, Katie, and Megan. Your insights, observations, and commitment to the study were priceless. What you got out of it proved again, as Hebrews 4:12 says, "For the Word of God is alive and active. Sharper than any double-edged sword, it penetrates even to the dividing soul and spirit, joints and marrow; it judges the thoughts and attitudes of the heart." Thank you to my patient, and encouraging, formatting wizard, Jodi McPhee, whose eye and creativity brought warmth and flowing beauty to the already beautiful words of Psalm 23. And of course, my devoted husband Steve: my biggest fan and cheerleader always.

OTHER BOOKS BY ROXANNE DRURY
- *Beyond the Blue Heaven Waits for You*
- *An Angel Named Glori*
- Coming Soon: *Glori's First Assignment*

Visit **roxannedrury.com** or **glorylandbooks.com**
for more information and to download free resources.

Contact me at: **glorylandbooks@gmail.com**
Facebook: **roxanne.drury.1**

Manufactured by Amazon.ca
Acheson, AB

15677648R00022